THE AMERICANA
COLORING BOOK

COLOR YOUR WAY ACROSS THE U.S.A.

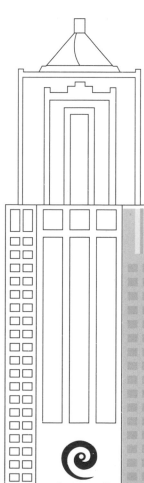

chartwell
books

EXPLORE THE LAND OF OPPORTUNITY, FROM SEA TO SHINING SEA!

Whether you're looking to walk down a childhood memory lane or you want to celebrate all things about Main Street, U.S.A., *The Americana Coloring Book* has all the classic and iconic imagery you'd expect from coast to coast, just waiting to be colored in. From bandshells and big tops to parades and, of course, the Stars and Stripes, this coloring book is designed to help you unwind and get coloring to explore your own personal creative side.

So what *is* Americana? As the name implies, it encompasses things associated with the culture, history, and people of America. It conjures a retro vibe of family friendly pastimes, with no shortage of red, white, and blue.

Just as there is no right or wrong way to express admiration for the Land of Opportunity, there is no right or wrong way to use this book. You can color in these beautiful illustrations however you wish and in whatever way feels right to you. This is about relaxing and getting in touch with what "Americana" means to you, whether that's famous landmarks and national parks or rodeos and rock & roll, so if one coloring page doesn't appeal to you, simply move on to one that does.

One of the great things about coloring is that it's accessible to anyone, regardless of artistic capabilities. Being able to add your own colors helps make it more personal, and there's no pressure to make these drawings perfect. So, turn the page for your particular slice of Americana and get coloring.

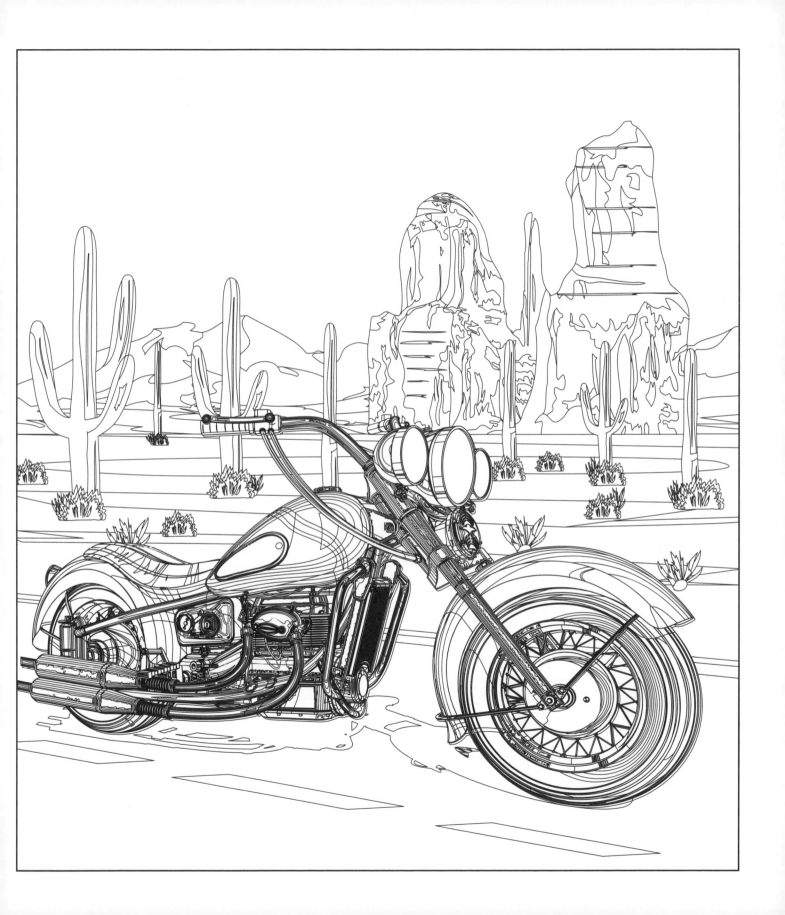

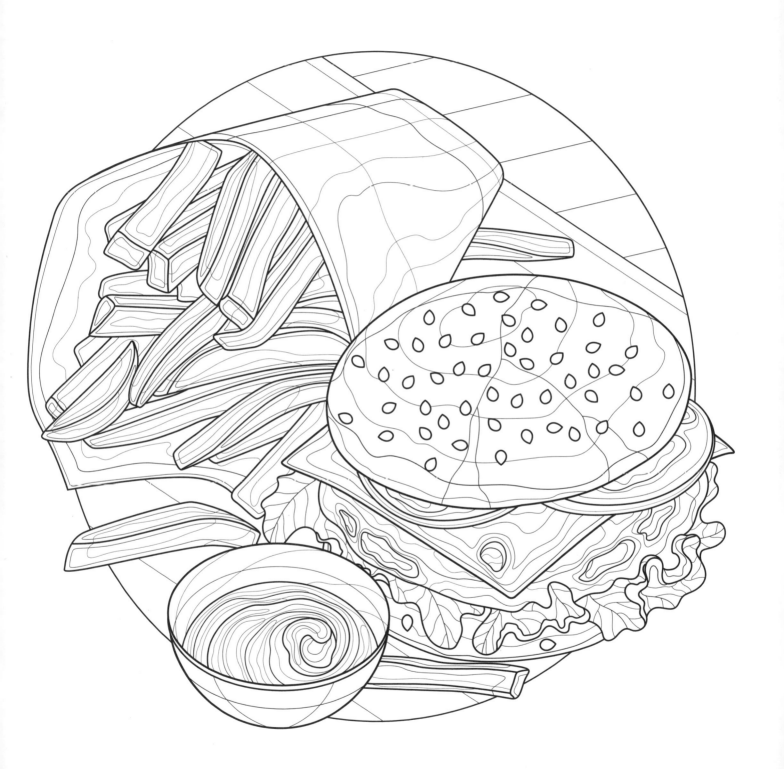

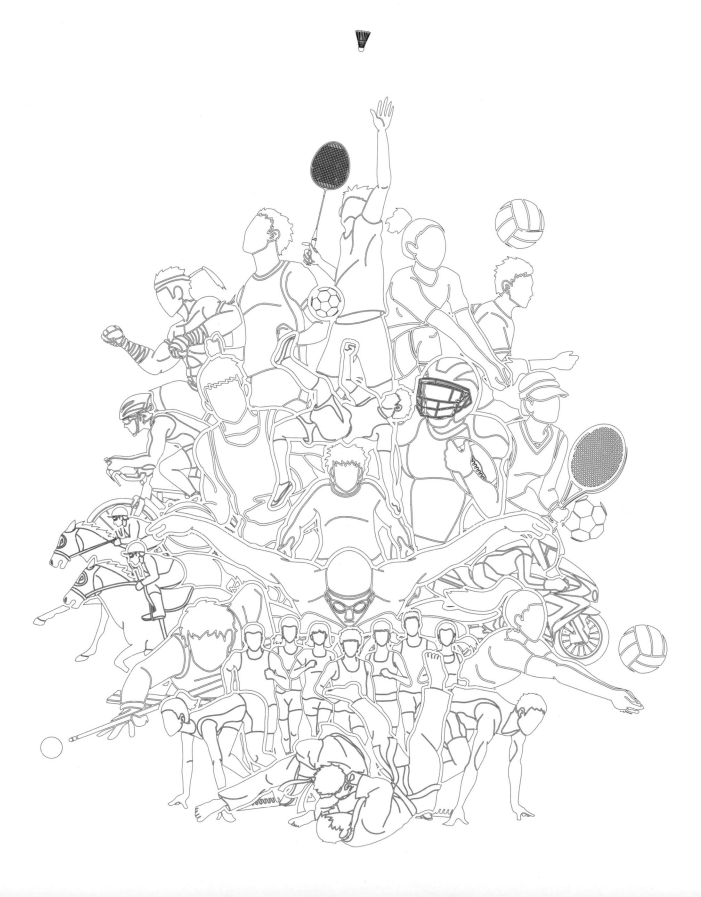

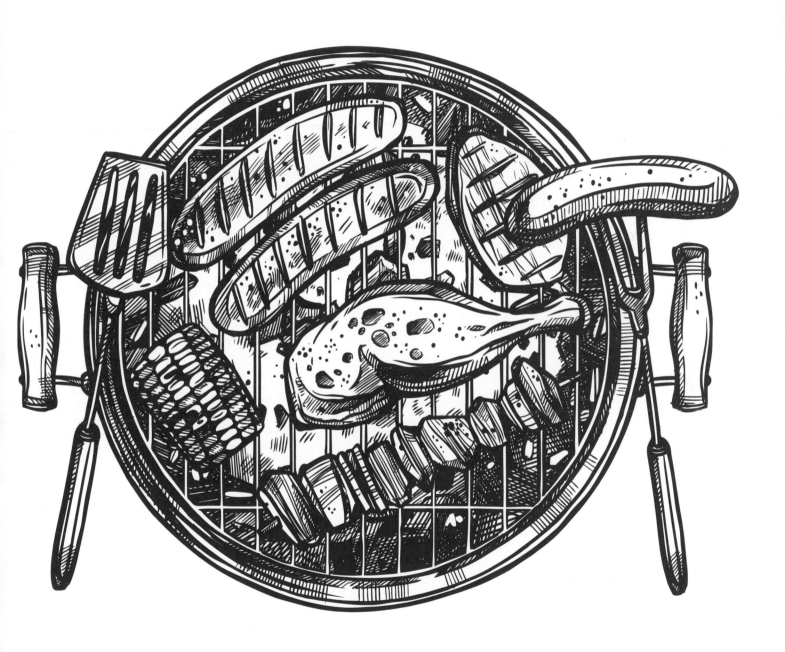

Quarto

© 2023 Quarto Publishing Group USA Inc.

This edition published in 2023 by Chartwell Books,
an imprint of The Quarto Group
142 West 36th Street, 4th Floor
New York, NY 10018 USA
T (212) 779-4972 F (212) 779-6058
www.Quarto.com

10 9 8 7 6 5 4 3 2 1

Chartwell titles are also available at discount for retail, wholesale, promotional, and bulk purchase. For details, contact the Special Sales Manager by email at specialsales@quarto.com or by mail at The Quarto Group, Attn: Special Sales Manager, 100 Cummings Center Suite 265D, Beverly, MA 01915, USA.

ISBN: 978-0-7858-4343-6

Publisher: Wendy Friedman
Senior Managing Editor: Meredith Mennitt
Senior Design Manager: Michael Caputo
Designer: Sue Boylan and Alana Ward
Editor: Jennifer Kushnier
Image credits: Shutterstock

Printed in China